BETWEEN EBB & FLOW

A LUMINESCENT LOVE

VOL. III

BY

SHANKARAN MALINI

BLUEROSE PUBLISHERS
India | U.K.

Copyright © Shankaran Malini 2024

All rights reserved by author. No part of this publication may be reproduced, stored in a retrieval system or transmitted in any form or by any means, electronic, mechanical, photocopying, recording or otherwise, without the prior permission of the author. Although every precaution has been taken to verify the accuracy of the information contained herein, the publisher assumes no responsibility for any errors or omissions. No liability is assumed for damages that may result from the use of information contained within.

BlueRose Publishers takes no responsibility for any damages, losses, or liabilities that may arise from the use or misuse of the information, products, or services provided in this publication.

For permissions requests or inquiries regarding this publication, please contact:

BLUEROSE PUBLISHERS
www.BlueRoseONE.com
info@bluerosepublishers.com
+91 8882 898 898
+4407342408967

ISBN: 978-93-6452-359-2

Cover design: Shivam
Typesetting: Namrata Saini
Images Credit: Freepik

First Edition: November 2024

SHANKARAN MALINI

BETWEEN EBB & FLOW
A LUMINESCENT LOVE

An Anthology of
Soulful Soliloquies

From the author of...

BOUND BY LOVE:
THE RED STRING OF FATE

&

LETTERS OF LOVE:
FROM ME TO THEE

For You...

They ask me... Who's this guy with russet brown eyes hidden in my poetry?

For whom these poems ooze out so much love...

Let me tell that... Again, and aloud...

You're my rhythm in every chord...

You're the meaning in every word...

Let me tell you that you're the one I love...

Let me tell you, all of this is for you...

And all of this is because of you...

For your eyes to see... And read...

And for your heart to feel... My heartbeat...

Thank You...

Foreword

FOR THE AUTHOR

In these pages, you'll find poetry that speaks to the very heart of love. With each verse, my dear friend Malini captures the rhythm of relationships—the highs and lows, the powerful surges and quiet retreats, just like the ocean's waves. Her words take us on a journey that goes beyond  mere feelings, touching the soul and reminding us that love is a force, ever-moving and alive. As you read, let yourself be carried by the ebb and flow of her words, and may you find reflections of your own heart within them.

BALAJI MANOHARAN

(A former colleague and friend of the author, Balaji is an entrepreneur. With roots in South India and now calling the U.K. home, Balaji leads Southern Trident, an organization dedicated to offering sustainable products to eco-conscious consumers. Driven by a passion for the environment and a curiosity to always learn and grow, he believes in going with the flow while making a positive impact on the world around him.)

A Word from The Author

We've all experienced it; there are days when we feel meh and then there are days when we feel yeah! And when in love, especially in a long-distance kind of love, it always happens—that feeling of voidness sometimes, missing your special someone, growing impatience until that next video call or the chime on your phone signalling those much-awaited messages. Then comes the dawning of maturity and understanding, finding happiness in seeing each other.

Nature embodies this pattern too, evident in the tidal cycles. It's said that in a day, there are two ebbs and two flows, and along with the moon's phases, these intensify. Love is also like that; what matters most is that through the ebbs and flows, highs and lows, love's vibrant luminescence always shines through.

This is the pattern you'll find in my Book 3, **Between Ebb & Flow: A Luminescent Love**. You'll read two ebb poems, filled with longing and yearning, and then two flow poems, brimming with overwhelming, overflowing love. At the end of these ebbs and flows, you'll find love's luminescence reflected in a colour—a hue that adds a magical glow to everlasting love, through the poet's heartfelt journey of discovering and embracing her true love. This poetic journey, narrated from the perspective of the poet, beautifully captures the essence of love's complexity and its enduring beauty.

Hope you enjoy sailing through these ebbs and flows, witnessing love's vibrant luminescence glow.

Happy reading! Between Ebb & Flow: A Luminescent Love

-Shankaran Malini - Author of Bound **by Love: The Red String of Fate** and **Letters of Love: From Me to Thee**

Thank You...

"Cultivate the habit of being grateful for every good thing that comes to you, and to give thanks continuously. And because all things have contributed to your advancement, you should include all things in your gratitude."
-Ralph Waldo Emerson

There's always and always something to be grateful for and when you start counting them as your blessings, you'll tend to lose count without even realizing it. My passion and determination have propelled me in all my poetic endeavours and I'm deeply for that inner drive that has always guided me.

I can't THANK YOU enough…

My mother, **Shrimathi Bhanumathy Shankaran**, my primary Guru and the person who taught me how to read and write - the alphabets, letters, and the language.

My loving father, **Shri TD Shankaran**, whose name I take great pride in prefixing before mine, who didn't hesitate or make any concessions to provide my sister and I with the best education.

My esteemed professors and instructors who believed in my potential and taught the language in a way that made me fall in love with it.

My most devoted fans, followers, and admirers, who have consistently shown their love and adoration for my poems and provided the most priceless and insightful feedback.

I want to express my gratitude to **Balaji Manoharan**, my friend and coworker, for writing the thoughtful FOREWORD to my book.

Rehan and Team at **Blue Rose One** who helped me shape this book.

My only and dearest little sister, **Revathi Shankaran**, for such a heartfelt AFTERWORD for my book. It means a lot to me, that you're there in my life.

*"But the love of sisters needs no words. It does not depend on memories, or mementos, or proof. It runs as deep as a heartbeat. It is as ever-present as a pulse."-**Lisa Wingate***

I'm An Endless Anthology
-A Prelude

You may think... I'm a petite poem...

Sometimes... Easy to comprehend...

Sometimes... Open to interpretation...

And... You call yourself my fan...

You know... You'll have to read between the lines...

Pause at the ellipses... Re-read... Linger around for long...

For... I'm an endless anthology...

When you choose to read...

You can never turn the pages quickly...

And you'll become addicted to me...

I'm a book you won't be able to put down.

Anthology

I'm Swirling in Your Russet Brown Eyes -Prologue 1
You Spoke to Me All Things Nice 2
I Miss You... A Little More Everyday 4
A New Love That's Meant Only for Me 5
Your Russet Brown Eyes 6
Yellow... Cause You're the One... 9
You're My Bosom Friend... You're My Ardent
Lover... 10
Will This Continually Spinning Earth Bring You
Closer To Me? 11
You're Navigating My Heart Right Through Its Line .. 12
You Know... I'm Very Sweet Too 13
Green... Is Life... Nurture... With Love 15
I Know You're Out There Somewhere 16
I'll Dream About You 17
You've Seized My Senses 18
My Love For You Is Raw... Wild... & Fierce... 19
Grey... I'll Love You in the Here and Now 20
Things Come to Life with Your Touch 22
Whatever Have You Done 24
You're An Effulgent Vortex 25

A Romantic Drive 26

Orange... The Colour of My Devotion for You 29

Where Our Hearts Align 30

Your Quiet's Sucking Out All of The Air I Breathe... .31

You're My Liminality... 32

You Love Me How I Love..33

White... Is My Love for You... 35

Between Stars..36

A Dialogue 37

You Linger in the Air Around Me..............................38

To My Man of All Seasons 39

Red... Is My Courage... To Love You... 41

You Exist Too Much in My Heart... In My Life... 42

You're The Drizzling Rain I Love to Soak In 43

I Want August to Reprise 44

I Feel Blissed in Your Name 45

Blue... Is The Truth... Bare 47

I Choose to Find Magic In You...................................48

You're Seemingly the One..49

I Can Smell Your Scent... All Over Me Already... 50

Your Heart Beats with A Kindness So Subtle 51

Pink... My Heart's Filling with You to The Brim.........53

My Love... What You're Turning Me into Really? 54

I Strongly Crave... To Get Inside Your Head 55

I Love You... And You Love Me 56

Now Please Tell Me... What Do I Write About? 59

Purple... In Me There's You Too 60

You Know... Where to Find Me... 61

Romantic Rainy Day 62

I'm Glad... You're Back Home... 63

You&I in the Here&Now 64

Dancing Peacock Green... New Beginnings 67

May The Primordial Feminine Divine Within...
-Postlude 68

Again&Again... Each Time... You Happen to Me
All Over...-Epilogue 69

Slowburn-An Endnote 70

Afterword 71

I'm Swirling in Your Russet Brown Eyes
-Prologue

I'm your captive... Swirling continually in your russet brown eyes...

My head's been spinning... With thoughts of you being on the other side...

Last night I slept like a baby... Like I know now what inner peace feels like...

And they all say... I'm glowing differently these days... And my smiles are infectiously bright...

I'm obsessing over you... And I care deeply for you...

Between the ebb and flow of my ever-growing love for you... My tender heart's longing to be closer to you...

You Spoke to Me All Things Nice

Was it really you? Or was it just my dream? Last night?
I can't describe...
You spoke to me... All things so sweet and nice...

"Hey beautiful... You're so pretty...
And you've such expressive eyes...
Somehow... I'm attracted to you...
Don't know why... Don't ask me why..."

"And I'm just getting to know you...
Your mischievous side...
Where your imaginations go wild..."

"You're indeed very special...
But... Please... Stop being so sweet... And humble..."

"I kinda miss you...
And this you need to know..."

I can't help smiling...
I can't stop blushing...
"Thankyou..." I said...

"Gratitude..." You said...
"Good night..." I said...
"Do you even think I can sleep tonight?" You asked...
I feigned a sleepy ignorance...
And then my eyes opened...
I ended up waking in my bed...

I Miss You...
A Little More Everyday

You've probably just woken up... In another part of the sphere...

Here I'm sleep deprived... And does this to you even matter?

Between your extremities of unbothered nonchalance and concerned care...

I feel slayed... Frantically swayed...

But you must be aware...

I'm missing you a little more... With each passing day...

A New Love That's Meant Only for Me

I'm every fragrant rose today...

The entire blooming garden's mine...

I'm all smiles...

And warm sunshine...

It feels like the onset of the very first spring in my life...

Perhaps it has come a little late...

Yet... 'Tis totally worth the wait...

Everything's so beautiful...

I just want this to last my entire lifespan...

And I can't keep calm...

When I see...

You've arrived...

With a love so new that's meant only for me...

I'm feeling so loved right now...

I'd vehemently rule out that roses have prickly thorns...

Your Russet Brown Eyes

Your russet brown eyes... Exude a kindliness...

They've opened for me... A portal to a parallel universe...

My heart's feeling happy...

For you've knocked on its chambers... Gently...

I've been breathing rather slowly... With a myriad emotions contained...

There's a heaviness... Betwixt us... Waiting to be unrestrained...

I'm awaiting the day... When love that exists... Between you and me...

Is uncamouflaged... And eventually revealed...

Your russet brown eyes... Are my only escapade... To find myself... Healed...

Yellow... Cause You're the One...

Yellow... The waxing crescent's up tonight...

Soon it'll be the moon's first quarter...

A golden sight...

Yellow... The mellow morning sunshine...

Raising hope against the odds...

Every single day...

The unwavering belief...

That you're mine...

Yellow... Tall smiling sunflowers, follow the sun,

Golden glow shines through my aura,

I'm in love with you...

Cause you're the one…

You're My Bosom Friend...
You're My Ardent Lover...

I wish you a good day...

My beloved dear...

The sun's risen... Where you're...

May you rise and shine... As always...

And out here...

It's the moon's first quarter tonight...

Gawking straight at my face...

I wonder... 'Whatever are you doing right here?'

'Aren't you in love with the sun?'

'And missing all the fun...'

Of being together?'

Like I'm missing You...

Right now... Right here...

I realize... Deep down in my heart...

And I feel it deep... Through my skin... In my bones...

You're my bosom friend... And You're my ardent lover...

Will This Continually Spinning Earth Bring You Closer To Me?

My brave heart's always been the toughest warrior on the fields...

Yet, so helpless and hopeless before you...

Suppressing everything it terribly feels...

Without the moon and the stars tonight...

These limitless skies seem so lonely...

Perhaps... There's bright sunshine where you're...

And out here the night's pitch dark...

Will this earth that's continually spinning...

Bring you closer to me?

It's not so much about the words in my verse tonight...

But it's all about feeling how my heart feels...

That I'm missing you a lot tonight...

Aren't you also missing me?

You're Navigating My Heart Right Through Its Line

I'll always remember this day...

When I invited you in...

And you've entered my life...

Forever to stay...

Bliss is you...

Bliss is in your beautiful name...

My heart's been ever growing fonder for you...

Because you're navigating my heart right through its line...

You've come as the gentle rain from the heavens...

And ever since...

Bliss is the eternal state I'm in...

I'll always remember this day...

For the rest of my life...

I'll always remember us this way...

A poem... That we're slowly becoming...

From two rhythmic lines...

You Know... I'm Very Sweet Too

"Chocolates!" You exclaimed in delight,

As you opened the gift box.

"You really like chocolates, don't you?" I asked,

As you nodded a 'Yes', I was absorbing the gleam in your eyes.

And I continued, "It's my favourite too,

Especially the bittersweet taste of these dark chocolates for its flavour."

Sobering up, you asked, "Hey, this is a lotttt.

Did you keep some for yourself at all? Or have you given away all?"

I paused for a split second, "As you savour these favourite chocolates of mine,

I'll also savour the irresistible sensation of chocolate melting in my mouth."

"So, would you like to share some?" You continued.

"Of course, and why not?" I said filled with glee, "It's so very sweet of you. But, you know, I'm very sweet too."

Green... Is Life... Nurture... With Love...

Green... The bangles on my hands jangle...
Your name on my lips, makes me smile...
The holy basil, in my small courtyard...
I grow and worship, sanctifies my heart...
My love for you, is a forest evergreen...
Stretching for several miles...
Green... This earth, your home and mine,
The grass I tread on, reminds me all the time,
Wishing on every star in the sky, that you'll be mine...
This abode has got my back all the while...
Green... The very last leaf I'll hold on to...
Be it snow or storm or shine...
Green... Is life... Nurture... With love...
I'm in love... Being your love... Beloved Valentine...

I Know You're Out There Somewhere

And I've been walking this earth long enough

Coz, I know you're out there somewhere...

I've hung the moon... And all the stars...

I've touched the horizons... And merged all shores...

And stitched the polars...

But are you so out of this world?

That I haven't yet been able to find you anywhere...

I'll Dream About You

'Tis Friday evening...

And the sun's setting...

At its own sweet pace...

It won't be too long until night...

My mobile phone screen dims out...

And dark theme's automatically turned on...

I look up your picture on socials...

And your most recently seen...

I feel a weird tingling within, as I look on...

The run up to the weekend...

Seems like an ambling journey...

And, as though gearing up for a montage movie...

I'll dream about you all through...

As if 'twere a lifetime...

You've Seized My Senses

Right now... And in this moment that I'm... It feels like I've known you for eons...

With you by my side... Everyday... I live in joy... Where happiness forever resides... In trillions of tons...

The closer... And closer... I get to you... The deeper... And deeper... In love with you I fall...

I'm a feral flower... Blooming unceasingly... Through the seasons all...

You've seized my senses... You've watered my withered heart with your kindness...

I'd give you everything you ask for... My eyes, my bile, and all of my years...

But I also want to live with you... All of my past lives... Every single moment in the present... And all of my future ones too...

And I want to make up for every lost nanosecond with you together...

My Love For You Is Raw... Wild... & Fierce...

I've been growing on you...

Little by little... Day by day...

But I'm not gonna tell you...

Right away...

I want this feeling to fill up my nerves to burst...

Swell up my lungs and pierce...

I want to savor it slowly...

My flesh and bones transpierced...

I've been growing on you...

My love for you is raw, wild and fierce...

But if I don't tell you right away...

My heart'll explode...

My eyes filled with a frenzied thirst...

Grey... I'll Love You in the Here and Now

Grey... Lumbering clouds... Hugging the horizons... Are holding up so much... In the welkins high...
You spoke some nice words... So did I...
And, a lot remains unsaid, still...
Candid... Behind those sparkling eyes...
Let's just spill our hearts out...
Like the downpour from the skies...
Grey... Ashes cannot be burnt again...
For eons and eons... Dear Soulmate... We've risen again...
Our paths have crossed... Once again...
We've found each other... Destiny has aligned...
Here we are... You and I...
I love you... I always have... I always will...
And forever... I'll love you, in the here and now...

Things Come to Life with Your Touch...

That teal shirt...

With full sleeves...

Wraps around you and tightly hugs!

Your majestic hairy chest...

That parfum odour...

With subtle oceanic notes...

Clings to your rugged body...

For such longer hours!

That mobile phone...

Entices you all through...

Feeling the tips of your fingers...

And in your ears - What does it constantly whisper!

Why doesn't it even for a while, leave you alone...

That bouquet of red roses...

And that one - My book of poems...

Being so gently held by you - In your hands...

Becoming your eye candy...

Smilingly making your eyes happy!

I'm filled with envy...

Of them all... That so sensually come to life with your touch...

And that chocolate, especially - Lures you in... For a soft bite of your lips!

Tempestuously melting, it gives up... Willing to get crushed under your teeth!

Whatever Have You Done

Whatever have you done,

In your pursuit, I've left everything behind.

I'm a wild chaotic mess, unfastened;

From becoming very caring, above and beyond,

To a fearlessness and strength that resonates with the mind;

Loving you as a whole,

Is something simply beyond my control.

You're An Effulgent Vortex

You're a free-spirited force,

Owning every place you go.

A soft-hearted soul,

One that cannot be yoked.

You're an effulgent vortex,

Radiating light and warmth all along.

It's the way you're - earthly and complex,

I'm simply carried away,

By you - my safest place - my home.

A Romantic Drive

And... You asked me... That evening... As we drove together... In your white car...

"So... What would you like to do next?"

I could think of so many things to say... Bizarre...

You'd be perplexed...

'Let's just keep going on this highway... Till this vehicle runs out of fuel... And we're stranded on a no-man's land...

How nice would it be, if this moment... Isn't fleeting anymore... And lasts a lifetime...

'Tis the golden hour... And the skies are turning blue... How about that you and I open our hearts...

Okay, now... I'm not getting out of your car... No matter what...'

And then... As though you read my mind... But feigning that you didn't.... You asked me again...

"So... What's your plan?"

Giving in, I said, "I'd like to go on a long drive with you... Do you've the time?"

And you smiled...

Orange... The Colour of My Devotion for You

Orange... Colour of the infant sun at dawn...
The shade of the sunset skies...
The mood of the marigolds in the garden...
My favourite citrus trees and the airs alkaline...
Orange... Hues of the autumnal...
The spirit of the spiritual...
'Tis energy...
A passion fiery...
Beloved Dear... 'Tis the colour of my devotion...
A heart, full of love... For you...
A soul... And it's deep longing for your connection...

Where Our Hearts Align

My mind's going a million miles an hour...

Your thoughts' lashing in... Hither and thither...

My heart's growing bigger...

Love for you filling in... More... And deeper...

My soul's growing older...

You're becoming familiar...

I keep walking... One foot in front of the other...

Hoping to meet you midway out there... Amid serendipitous encounters...

Where our hearts align... And our souls recognise each other...

Your Quiet's Sucking Out All of The Air I Breathe...

You don't notice... How my heart opens...

As the flower does in its blooming hour.

You fail to listen...

My screams into the storm... That, I'm a burning tower...

If blood flows through your heart... How come you don't my gush feel...

Your quiet's sucking out all of the air I breathe... And you just can't be doing this to me...

You're My Liminality...

Somewhere... Between day and night...

You're that flickering hope of mine...

Sometimes hours feel like minutes...

And sometimes a moment feels like a lifetime...

Joy ridin' on the highway of this earthly heaven...

You're those little detours... And my destination...

Between wakefulness and sleep...

You're my consciousness... That exists... A liminality...

Between who I was and who I want to be...

You're... My now... My reality...

You Love Me How I Love

I live by everyday happiness...

Waking up just to see the orange sun...

Wishing a good day ahead to everyone...

Staying up with the moon under the starry vastness...

What the small pleasures of life feel like...

Winging in waves... Walking barefoot on green grass...

Being kind... Making someone smile...

The feeling on my skin when I see how happiness fills someone's eyes...

I'm just an everyday brunette...

I believe in magic and miracles... Dreams and guardian angels...

That pull of the heart... And feeling of the gut...

I believe in the sway of infectious love...

Just the same way... I believe... You love me how I love...

White... Is My Love for You...

White... Colour of the intensely fragrant jasmine blooms...
Manna, which infants drool...
Dreamy cover of snow...
On paths untrodden, and peaks unknown...
Fluffy clouds hovering the skies...
Unlocking diviners' visions foretold...
White... Is bright... Light...
Where all colours in the spectra blend...
White... Is peace eternal... Pure and ethereal...
My love for you... Deep... Knows no end...

Between Stars...

You tell me, "Will connect with you soon..."

And I'm filled with glee.

Indeed, I look forward to the day

In anticipation, excitedly.

And, as if

Your words of hope

Have landed me between stars,

I don't see the dark.

Rather, a path, sure,

That leads to you,

The one who completes my arc...

A Dialogue

"I'm afraid... I may become vulnerable, around you...," you say...

"You're... The wild feminine...

The unstoppable waters... That can't be contained...

The fire, I'm tempted to touch...

The freezing cold ice, I want to tightly hug...

Your words make me smile... As I read between the lines...

It has never happened thus before... Today... You're inciting the divine masculine..."

And then, your stark silence, begins looming over my skies...

Like pregnant clouds, awaiting to burst open on my soil...

I'm afraid... I'm becoming vulnerable with you... All these things that you say and do...

I don't like roaming around much... And now I can't stay still anymore...

It has never happened thus before... I'm tempted to wanderlust... Your dense beard grove's now my maze to explore...

You Linger in the Air Around Me...

At times... This sudden feeling... Of the warm wind, tickling my skin...

Makes me perspire, as though... Your breath has just touched my chin...

I feel you... Linger in the air, around me...

I look you up, on my mobile phone... I see... You're online...

Are you also thinking about me?

Stringing verses together... Line by line... Our wedding invitation wordings...

Fragrant flowers... Radiant smiles... Sacred vows... Golden hour... Wedding bells pealing...

Destined with you... This day... Every single day... This entire lifetime... Before and beyond... I'm your beautiful bride...

Tis a feeling magical... Miracles are real...

I'm living my dream... My eyes open wide...

You've just viewed my poem... Wrote a comment and posted a like...

To My Man of All Seasons

I love you... With a madness... That totally loves this feel of love, that doesn't reason,

I love you... With a fearlessness fierce... That doesn't fear whether at all you'll love me in return,

I love you... As the wilderness wild... For you're... My Man of all seasons...

Red... Is My Courage... To Love You...

Red... You're hand holding, a bunch of roses,
In my favourite picture of you,
My incessant blushing, in joy and coy... Standing right here, in front of you,
Red... Blessed vermilion... Your love is my dream come true... Brightening up my lifetime...
A bit of it, falls on my nose, as you apply on my hairline...
Red... You're my passion, my desire... The blood running through my veins...
The courage to love you... In every way, every day... Gorgeously... Saying your name...

You Exist Too Much in My Heart... In My Life...

The moon's hardly illuminated tonight...

What's been blocking all of its light?

I can't stop feeling anxious right now...

My mind's been overthinking all the 'why' and 'how'...

For you've also been so quiet...

Has the moon conspired with you... to play seek and hide?

This heaviness is pitch dark... it ain't invisible...

Nor is it something that can be passed in silence...

Because... it's a truth so tangible...

You exist too much... in my heart... in my life...

You're the forever full moon in my skies...

You're The Drizzling Rain I Love to Soak In

I don't crave your reassurance every day,

In words sugary or infallible presence.

You're way too precious to me in every meaning,

Oh, my heart's chosen one.

For you aren't just a love mundane,

Your existence in my lifetime is and will always be special.

You're the drizzling rain I'll always love and dare to soak in,

As much as your genteel sprinkles through my window pane.

I Want August to Reprise

The 'Ber' months are almost here...

Today's still the last day of August...

And 'twas just like yesterday...

Nine days into the eighth month this year...

When you and I found each other...

I feel lost and found...

Ever since, in the woody wilderness of your russet brown eyes...

I just can't let the moment slip away...

Without knowing what lies ahead...

In the tapestry of time as we tread...

And in every other month, here on, I want August to reprise...

I Feel Blissed in Your Name

September...

Is beginning to sink in... My skin...

Days are getting shorter...

And I'm getting the inkling...

You and I are coming closer than ever...

And this joy in my heart... Knows no bounds...

For there's only happiness... I see... All around...

I feel blissed in your name... Your russet brown eyes make my world go round...

The Ber months are caving in oceans... And merging timelines...

To bring forth the day of our wedding, where your heart and mine will intertwine...

Blue... Is The Truth... Bare

Blue... I know... Is your favourite hue...

The colour of the same skies we share...

I close my eyes... And see the oceans wide... No shores in sight...

I see blue... Everywhere...

I smell you...

Blue... Is bliss... Blue... is bold... Blue... Is soothing...

And blue... Is the truth... Bare...

That... In my love for you... I've found my soul's calling…

I Choose to Find Magic In You

Ah! The waning crescent's up in the night skies...

And the mind's spiralling between ebb and flow,

Through the tides...

I'm brave... Then why's it that sometimes I'm afraid?

Looks like I've really come a long way in this...

That I forget why do I love you so much in the first place...

That even when I don't have control over my overthinking mind,

I truly feel very happy seeing your face...

I'm a big believer in magic... And that it exists...

And I choose to find it in your warm embrace...

You're Seemingly the One

You... Sometimes...

Terrify me...

With your warmth... And cold...

All at the same time...

My mind tends to overthink...

And my legs start to slow down...

Feeling terribly weak...

My tender heart's unable to fathom...

Whatever's happening with me...

You're seemingly the one...

As the lover...

And my bosom friend...

You familially surprise me...

And then you give me the chills... Down my spine...

Becoming the distant stranger... Unrecognisably...

And in all this... I can never bring myself to undo...

What my heart's already done...

I Can Smell Your Scent...
All Over Me Already...

I can read your mind... Clearly... Through your quiet...
And words minimalistic...

And... I can feel you deeply... Through your emoji smiles...
And subtle pauses...

And the more I do...

I like you even more... I just can't help falling for you...

My curious eyes... Visualise...

And my heart's set ablaze...

By your countenance handsome...

Wearing a Dallas moustache...

That petite goatee... And those sensual sideburns...

My prying ears... Wonder...

Your masculine voice... As a fireplace live...

That keeps my inner soul thoroughly wired...

And I can smell your scent...

All over me...

Already...

It's one of a kind...

That comes once in a life... And lasts a lifetime...

I'm restless... Awaiting you... Soonly...

To reveal yourself to me...

Your Heart Beats with A Kindness So Subtle

I've always thought... I've been through suffering... For reasons unfair... Whatsoever...

And that's probably why I'm not like the others...

Then... I met you...

Wondering what was so different... About you... That I'll know...

I was completely blown away...

By your swelled heart... That's witnessed... All the way...

And still healing... From loss... And love disguised as grief... Irreplaceable...

Yet beats with a kindness so subtle...

And ever since... My entire world's been flipped... My feelings for you gradually losing control...

And that's the exact moment... I realized...

I'm falling in love with you... Deeply... Body... Heart....And soul...

Pink... My Heart's Filling with You to The Brim

Pink... Cherry blossoms bloom in the spring...

My heart's filling with you to the brim...

Pink... I'm craving roses esculent...

To palate your love in all its sweetness so eloquent...

Pink... My cheeks turn on feeling the tickles...

Cause you're desirably irresistible...

Pink... Our bundle of joy... Where happiness knows no bounds...

Our daughter... Dearest... Loving... Angel... Darling... Our life's now come to a full circle round...

My Love... What You're Turning Me into Really?

I've been totally preoccupied... Lately...

With you permeating... My memory and my whole being... Steadily...

You're making me very, very desperate... And you're training my patience...

My love... What you're turning me into, really?

I don't know how much of this lifetime is still left for me...

I very sincerely wish... To make every moment count with you...

May the heavens come down... In the way you love me wholeheartedly...

I Strongly Crave... To Get Inside Your Head

I could just keep talking with you...

Through sunrises and sunsets...

Under every crescent moon swing that'll be hung up in the skies blue...

A lifetime wouldn't ever be ample...

And an eternity wouldn't be endless too...

But... I like listening to you...

More than anything else...

Decoding intently every 'Hmmm' and 'Mmm' you say...

Through your non-silent pauses...

I strongly crave... To get inside your head...

And play all the thoughts and words for me you've stored therein...

That you're still waiting to share…

I Love You... And You Love Me...

You're pulling me closer... And closer...

I'm the wild ivy creeper...

Your outstretched arms... Become the huge shady tree...

With branches laden with flowers and green leaves...

And I'm entwining around you... Completely...

You also liberate me... By letting me be...

You're the majestic mountain tall... And I'm the dancing waterfall...

Flowing incessantly... Unravelling through the steeps...

And that's the way it is...

Our love story...

I love you... And you love me...

Now Please Tell Me... What Do I Write About?

This morning felt so different...

Like I'm no longer living this life alone...

I'm sharing it with a special someone...

And if joy were a fruit... I've been picking them up...

Ever since... My basket's been overspilling... And at this rate, I wouldn't ever be done...

I haven't been able to believe my eyes... I finally see you...

And that we spoke and shared loads at length...

And now when everything's right there before my eyes...

What's even left to my imagination?

Now please tell me... What do I write about?

This whole new feeling... That's there for you... Heartfelt and true...

And my ever-growing affection... For you...

Purple... In Me There's You Too

I'm drawn towards purple hues...
'Tis a beautiful blend...
Of my favourite colour... Red...
And... Your favourite colour... Blue...
When golden hour turns magical...
Under the breathtaking lilac skies...
Along the wavy terrains of the alluring lavender...
I dare to dream with open eyes...
Somewhere in me... There's you too...
Whenever, and wherever... You see purple hues...
You'll find me right there, next to you...

You Know...
Where to Find Me...

You know me...

On some days, I stay up all night, and sleep through the day;

On some days, I'm up early... And when night comes, I sleep like a baby.

There are days when I'm happy... And then on some days, I'm angry...

There are some days when I'm chatty... And then on most days, I'm all poetry...

Sometimes, I'm just a frenzied flame... And sometimes, I'm all tranquillity, my Eternal Flame...

I do have my highs and lows... Ebbs and flows...

I've various terrains within... Snow fields to ski through... Deserts to explore... Mountains to climb and oceans several to swim...

There's an entire universe inside me...

My Beloved Dear... You know me... Deeply...

And you know when, where, and how to find me...

Romantic Rainy Day

I woke up to the pitter patter of raindrops...

This misty morning is like straight out of a dream...

I fancy scribbling on those foggy windows...

So, I draw a heart, and a four-leaf clover... And I write our names...

This thing feels surreal... It feels so good...

Everything just feels so right...

This earthy aroma accompanying the rain...

Nature's mocktail is getting me high...

And then my phone chimes...

I know you're right here...

And that the magic is real...

I'm Glad... You're Back Home...

You were away... Briefly...

My heart pounded against my rib cage impatiently...

I couldn't feel my soul in my body...

There was a void I failed at filling badly...

I'm glad... Today, you're back home...

My breath has been restored in my lungs...

If sometime you plan to go somewhere again...

Please... Don't ever leave me here alone...

You&I in the Here&Now

Maybe... I came into this world rather hurriedly...

I was born a two-week premature baby...

All these years, I've been walking this earth... Looking for someone...

Until the moment happened... When I knew you're the one...

My heart felt heavy... When I realised, you're out there already...

Just when I moved closer to where you're... Why did the sacred red thread we're bound by took you oceans afar...

Year after year I've wandered... Picking myself up again whenever I faltered...

And that's why... This hour... This quietude... The moon and all the stars and the sprawling skies to me immensely matter...

You and I... In the here and now... And there's no latter...

Dancing Peacock Green... New Beginnings

I know... You've been holding back...

Like the grey and dense clouds...

Your mind is trying to reason...

But your heart already knows...

What your body's burning with desire for...

I want you to know... I'm right here...

Waiting... For you...

Let go of your fears...

Open your heart...

Like the skies clear...

The dancing peacock green... Awaits...

Strutting... Into new beginnings with grace...

Spreading out... Iridescent blue and green plumage...

Dear Soulmate... The path to real love this... Let's embrace...

May The Primordial Feminine Divine Within... -Postlude

May the burning desires within, be those meant to become,

May what you dare to dream turns real for good,

May what you believe in, never ever let you down,

May words be verses, that'll stay evergreen,

May every colour in the world, fill you up with love that never loses sheen,

May you stay whole, through every phase, be it light or dark, just like the moon,

May the Primordial Feminine Divine within...

Lead the heart... To where it will belong...

Again&Again... Each Time... You Happen to Me All Over... -Epilogue

For I wouldn't just settle for any other,

For I asked for better,

The best that could happen to me ever.

For I choose to patiently wait,

No matter how long it takes,

For I'm a believer in the red string of fate.

For no matter what path, I walk on, and the detours,

For wherever I go, whatsoever,

Again and again, each time you happen to me, all over.

Slowburn-An Endnote

You can't read me... Like an open tome...

But I do want you to know me...

You'll have to lose yourself in me... Completely...

Unlearn to learn...

You can't love me... All at once...

You'll have to let yourself fully savour...

Every single moment with me...

This chemistry that there is... Between you and me...

Is a slow burn...

Afterword

FOR THE AUTHOR

*"We write to taste life twice, in the moment and in retrospect." -**Anaïs Nin***

All of life is a montage of moments. Most of those moments are the daily grind of lethal routine… and then like a bolt from the blue or something less dramatic like a flower blossoming or a butterfly fluttering come moments that are too special and too surprising for words. This anthology is much like a bouquet of these choice moments with one significant difference… they are embellished by words. Words of an author, of a daughter, a sister, a lover, a liver who has the gift of expression and articulation… who can be expressive even where many would be ineffable.

For those who don't know her personally, the author is best described as a quiet, efficient, meticulous and thorough professional, a soldier in the army of superwomen who balance work and life. In her journalism days I have seen her type a 500 word breaking story as multiple text messages on a standard phone (no iPhone or Pixel those days) to ensure the story made it to press on time. I have also seen her attend meetings and work on press releases till late night and wake up in the morning for another round of deliverables with the same gusto and energy! As a student or as a professional her commitment to being fully present in the moment, to soak in all the information and experiences it presents, these have been her biggest strength and her secret sauce to finding the right words for the right moments.

"I am what I am. Doing what I want to do. Expressing myself as I feel I should." - ***James Baldwin***

So Malini is one who won't demonstrate her emotions openly, and certainly not in a setting of in LinkedIn parlance-2nd or 3rd connections. But that doesn't mean that the emotions are absent. They simmer in some labyrinth of her heart and mind and effortlessly find their way out when pen meets paper. Each of these poems is a glimpse into that impervious persona and the feelings within, that are too deep, too simple for words. I wish her professor Dr Nalini Prabhakaran could see in form what she knew years before when she read one of this bard's earlier poems to say …" still waters truly run deep!"

"How many loves do you think there are?

There are as many kinds of love as there are shades of colour in the universe, and most of us are blind to them all."
-Erin Van Vuren

In Malini's world there are as many types of love as there are shades of colour in the universe. And she knows them all. Which is how she can express 30 different flavours of gratitude to the most important people in her life. Which is how she can be blown by the simple faith of her toddler nephew in God. Which is how she can have a conversation with her imagined daughter. Which is how she can ruefully reflect on how the roles have reversed between parents and daughter where the daughter becomes the parent to her child-like father and mother.

As Paulo Coelho said "[love] isn't what romantic songs tell us it is—love simply is." I believe the author has captured this deep yet simple essence of love in all her poems. I also hope that this anthology lends words to your feelings and guides you to communicate in the form that you are most comfortable with. Because "love not said is love not felt".

Happy reading!

REVATHI SHANKARAN

(Apart from being my lil sister and partner in crime, Revathi is a Sr Communications Manager in the office of the SVP for Infrastructure and Cloud Services in Cisco and a Proud mom of a lovely son and daughter}.

www.ingramcontent.com/pod-product-compliance
Lightning Source LLC
LaVergne TN
LVHW041539070526
838199LV00046B/1749